TRACIN

TRACING
THE UNSPOKEN

BY MILAN ŠELJ

TRANSLATED BY THE AUTHOR AND HARVEY VINCENT

BODY LANGUAGE

A MIDSUMMER NIGHT'S PRESS

New York

This book was printed with the support of
Trubar Foundation at the Slovene Writers' Association, Ljubljana, Slovenia.

Original title: *Slediti neizgovorjenemu*, published by ŠKUC-Lambda, 2018.

Cover image by Stefano Cipollari.

A Midsummer Night's Press
3 Norden Drive
Glen Head NY 11545
amidsummernightspress@gmail.com
www.amidsummernightspress.com

Grateful acknowledgment is given to the editors of
The Queer Riveter, where some of these poems appeared.

Designed by Nieves Guerra.

ISBN-13: 978-1-938334-38-2
First edition.

The author wishes to express his profound gratitude to Harvey Vincent, translator, collaborator and friend, for his invaluable help, encouragement and support. This book is for you, dear Harvey.

The author also wishes to express his appreciation and thanks for the editorial and proofreading help by the editor Lawrence Schimel.

Desire without a body is the hollow call of a fallen animal. Wounded, it lies in a thicket, licking its genitals. In the valley I hear a stag barking.

I was getting hungry and impatient. At the train station, I wandered aimlessly in careful circles and drew awkward lines amidst the crowds of people on the platform. To avoid their inquisitive eyes, I ignored the passers-by. Could I catch some quick excitement before the departure of a train?

He mesmerized me with his gaze and I followed him. In broken English he managed to explain where his car was parked. He offered me a seat for the night and I reluctantly took it. Before we fell asleep he wanted money. When I told him I didn't have any, he punched me in the face. The spray from my bloody nose stained his shirt. Then he really lost it. *You will pay for this tomorrow* he screamed as he ripped the shirt to shreds, then landed his fist on my battered head.

I was picked up by an older chap with a notepad. In the taxi he kept insisting he wasn't gay. He wanted to find out what *boys of my kind* did for money. I'd heard it all before and knew exactly what he wanted. In his faded little flat I lay on a table among the remains of stinking food and dirty glasses. I kept squeezing my nipples so I would come quickly. Then I picked 20 quid from his fucking pocket.

He lures me to the church loft where he wants to show me a convex baroque ceiling. Or so he says. In the bell tower, behind the wooden fence, he pins me with his look, pushing me against the wall with his foot. The buttons are no obstacle for his swift hand. My own slides lower with the metal zipper. I smell sweet milky chestnut, while his quick trembling breath tickles my neck. At home my trouser leg betrayed me, stained with sticky drops.

I don't remember when I last saw a cheap salami, spring onions and a bottle of vodka on his table. *Shall we have something to eat?* my companion says. *I'm hungry*, I say. *So, let's feast*, he barks, *but first I'll take off my boots.* With a mischievous laugh he pulls his shorts up even higher, wolfs down his grub and snarls: *Did you really think I would feed you for free, you fucking nitwit?*

Even when I feel cold biting at my feet, I don't give up. In this hollow space where I now live, I'm pushed against a steep wall. My cage is a hanging trap without windows or doors. I keep going because I need to capture the light. Where I came from, I was never allowed to look out. In this desolate country I must always struggle to look in.

Idiots promise us *Heaven on Earth*. My passion was always stronger than the chains that tied me to a rock. I fought every obstacle. Fear ravaged my gut with unfathomable sounds. Winter is merciless. Its icy shell restricts until the umbilical cord is cut. From the thaw spring bursts free.

The last flakes of light are melting at one end of an unmade bed. A henchman releases a single stroke as beads of perspiration drop onto another body. Flurries of anger lick the exposed face and neck of a terrified boy. I hardly breathe because I don't know who will be next. Dozing traitors rarely sleep.

I've been hanging around for ages in the twilight of these empty streets, expecting a hostile look at every corner. Will I ever tire of hiding the scars of my restlessness? Like others I search in darkness for some threshold that bids me welcome to an inner sanctum. Sometimes I get so close I'm almost there. Then a surging rip-tide drags me even further away.

Someone stealing through the rain interrupts my sleep. I can barely make out what he's murmuring: *Wake up! The river will rise so high that by morning we won't be able to wade through it.* Wind thrashes bare branches. Torn scraps of plastic hang in the air and I see patches of sky through the slits. Nobody's here and I'm alone. A steep cliff slopes down to a bridge leading nowhere.

Arabs brag they are the best, my friend, because they insist on being a top. Bulgarians get picked more often than Romanians because they are cheaper. Romanians are less choosy than Hungarians, you know, because they are always happy to be a top or a bottom. Nobody asks black guys anything, if you are lucky to find one for a fuck. But in the end, I say, we are all the same. The only difference is the price of a good lay.

He took the mandolin in his delicate hands. It was standing there forlorn and forgotten, leaning against a dusty bookshelf full of clutter. Aimlessly plucking the strings, he took a deep breath, plunged into himself and started to sing. His song was full of grief and ferocious anger. I trembled with excitement and fear.

I always believed what I wanted to believe and flattered myself that I loved you. Imagining that you loved me too, whenever I offered a substantial bribe. This was all fool's gold. We were strangers at a dead-end, fighting over a crown made of straw. My game was to gamble all or nothing. That's how much I needed you.

Master, please don't let me fall backwards like the fading light of silence. I polish your boots and let you walk carelessly on my toes. Every night I fluff up the blankets and lie naked next to you. Any punishment is more lenient than wordless forgiveness. Why do you disregard me so? Your burning look is losing its glow.

Silence suffocated language, so I listened to my inner child. Those strained membranes remember every single threat and angry glance. Breaking tectonic plates slide into the open, where everything revealed will not be forgotten. Never will I stop speaking to please you or my wounded vulnerable self.

He came to me downcast and dejected, without a trace of self-worth, which usually betrays incompetent thieves. Having fought with other pick-pockets for his miserable share of the loot, he lay next to me. His bandaged bleeding fist a soft rosebud squeezed between my thighs.

A shaved head is resting next to mine. I try to embrace his quick breath after the spill of burning sperm. Above the window sill, rays of sunlight slip through a slit in the curtains. Slowly, like an elegant jackal, he sneaks out of bed, leaving behind the impression of a sensuous shadow. I let him steal the last word before he departs. His sharp fragrance floats in the air, enveloping my still-quivering body.

In exchange for a few quid, he embraced me awkwardly when I brought him to my place and nervously undressed him with hungry eyes. He allowed me to kiss the two crescents of his closed eyelids and touch the birth-mark on his left shoulder. That was all I could get and I behaved like a guilty bastard stealing from a wretched beggar.

You knock on the door. I get the feeling you want to leave even before you properly enter. You make up all sorts of stories, then storm out. All afternoon you keep calling and sending hysterical messages. This time, instead of the usual evasions, you promise what you've never offered. How did you know I would eventually give you the keys, some change, and the peace and quiet of a nap on the sofa?

At dawn, he follows him into the woods. Hidden behind a magnificent trunk, he eavesdrops and shivers restlessly in anticipation of lust. There, among thick branches on soft moss, he catches sight of his elegant, hairy thigh. He grabs his beloved by the ear boldly. The young buck quickly vanishes into the enveloping forest, where wild desire stirs under stately elms.

The intensity of your presence excites the core of my being. You evade the babblings of this foolish old man, as I ignore your conceited scorn. My withered hands seek the warmth of your indifferent nakedness. I will follow you where hell's fire eats heaven's light and the touch of death will never reach us.

Around Christmas he became jittery and homesick. I bought him a pair of shoes, a one-way ticket and credit for his mobile phone. Standing at the window I waited for his call as I watched the first snowflakes. They always cover my restlessness with silence. I kept telling myself I was right to send him away. Will we be closer if he decides to come back?

He never got a single joke. When he spoke, Furies broke commas, disfigured adjectives and interrupted punctuation. He spit bitter sulphur and threatened to kill baby birds in the nest, maybe the feral cat too; hurting me with all sorts of provocations. How could he lick the scars of brutality they made him suffer? In such blistering confusion he did not know how to defend himself.

When will you return to the body, make peace with yourself, and cease this incessant rage? Your skin is mine and mine is yours. Isn't that what it says in the contract? Soon we will lie down. Old, exhausted and alone. The shudder of contempt gnaws at the bone, gaping at us from the abyss and depth of our being.

He offers to iron my trousers and get rid of the oil stain. We pack my suitcase and make sure there's enough food in the fridge. I leave money for him on the table. In the evening at the hotel I notice some bank notes in my wallet are gone. My sadness is greater than the missing amount. Why did he steal when all he had to do was ask?

You brought your accomplices with you. They were all high on *speed*, screaming with laughter, stealing from bookshelves and drawers like hungry magpies. Everything not glued to the wall or nailed to the floor – credit cards, cheque-book, PC and a new TV – they stole. During your shameless merry-making, you promised me *this* young stud or *that* one with the black spiky hair, when all I wanted was you.

He pulls up his *Calvin Klein* briefs, not worried about the fact they are fake. He thinks they're the *real thing*. Like him. I don't care about all this and let my pinkie finger slip under his waistband. *No entry*, he quietly orders. *No need to whisper, dear boy*, I tease him, *nobody can hear*. When I touch him, his eyebrows are tense, but his palm resting on my hip tells me he's still on the game.

Feeling dizzy, the odors of a new city linger in the air. I spot him sitting at a distant table. The morning sun splits his face into images of light and shade. Suddenly he turns and our eyes connect for a moment. Besotted in the presence of such beauty, I could not avert my gaze.

I'm clinging to my mobile. You never, ever call. I'd hoped you would stop punishing me. Even your sharp tongue is better than this damned silence. *Call me now. Please! No questions, I promise.* The screen remains dark and stubbornly mute.

I'm fucking fed up, he complains. We sit on our neglected balcony. The plants' leaves are sickly, yellowed by the sun and tobacco smoke. *To hell with everything*, he says and smashes a glass. The air is cold so we move to the kitchen. Down below, wearing patched up pullovers and thin winter coats, I see noisy children on their way to school. The morning light has faded and the landscape is bleak.

I will let you persuade me how insignificant the autumn is, but only when your belly is bursting with spring. Forget every single scruple about summer. Your thoughts shall deepen, your shoulders broaden and gather strength. In winter, when you're older, you will discover that doubt is the wellspring of life.

When I have plenty, I'm happy to give, I tell him, as I try to cling to his falling hand. *When I don't, I give a bit less.* He keeps quiet, but his bewildered look doesn't promise a gracious response. Like an idiot I realise I went too far in my expectations. I want something from somebody who has so little to give.

In the back seat of the car he mutters to himself: *Oh god, for the first time I think I'm falling in love with a man!* For a moment I find this confession banal. Do I detect a whiff of regret in his voice? Maybe he thinks he's been missing something. I whisper: *Lovey, don't worry, there's a first time for everything.*

Hands. Your betraying hands. They leave invisible traces everywhere. The touch of your palm is idle. Your knotted fists cover my mouth. I feel stifled, unable to scream. My blindness to your petty lust betrays me. Why don't you invade the space below, where I hide the remains of dread from a lost childhood? Come inside me then, if you dare.

Soft dark skin, broad shoulders and a mighty curvature are your best bargaining chips. Leading a free life in this fantasy jungle as a magnificent savage in a loin cloth, you stomp all over me.

I am not your baby Jane, Tarzan!

You think you need to go deeper into the entrails of a mysterious self and confront your demons? Do that some other time. Chase these raucous birds from tousled hair, lay your head on a hairless chest and let me give you love.

We were sitting on a bench at the bus stop. Our eyes interlocked, avoiding the stares of strangers and provoking them with our disdain. Later the descending road overtook the howling wind of disapproval. And if you'd said: *The day is only an inevitable contrast to the night*, I would have agreed. During the journey, our eyes sparkled with hints. The evening was a game of questions. You answered none of mine.

You have no idea how small this town is. Desperation is stifling and centuries old. Why don't you cut off your shirtsleeves and send them to me? I'll embrace myself with them when I'm not able to shorten your absence. To save myself, I'll search for consolation between the scraps of fabric and let your scent linger on the cuffs.

Sunday morning is glassy and the light is bitter. Blocks of flats built under the communists are magnified by the creaking of an old bus as it staggers on its way to the suburbs. Aimlessly, I end up at the Central Post Office. Through a window I try to imagine your face in the reflection. The breath on my lips is a measure of distance between you and me.

There's a letter downstairs, waiting for me by the front door. The address is written in square letters I recognise straightaway. Trembling, I hide the envelope under a pillow. In the evening I summon enough courage to open it. *As I write to you it is almost midnight. The two arms on the clock will soon be together. Like you and me.* For a moment I almost believe you. Your games are lies. Nothing but lies.

We went drinking that night, down by the harbor where smugglers used to gather. As usual, he was the loudest one in the joint. Smelling of *schnapps*, he spluttered and dribbled. Staggering alone across the paved courtyard, he asked passers-by for the way home. I ran behind him. It was too late. All that remained was the open sea.

Alone, I listen to the BBC. Your photo slips off the kitchen table. You stare at me from the floor, bewildered. On the radio, Mahler's *Kindertotenlieder* is interrupted. Does this pause in the music mark your disappearance in the measures of silence? The anguish in the singer's voice grows darker. I can barely make out your face in the twilight.

Shards of restlessness often overwhelm your encrypted messages, sent from the room behind the locked door. The key I use to open it is getting thinner. Although you constantly provoke me, in my dreams you never utter a single word. As if you were convinced sharp blades of grass had grown in my ears and I would never hear anything you have to say.

Every August you reappear. Memories of that summer night are like blossoms without perfume. I return to your room. Shelves are covered with rows of LPs. From a different space, your voice keeps haunting my music. Slowly you are teaching me how to listen and love.

In the bedroom, searching for signs of your shadow, I fold your worn-out socks, soft underwear, a woolly sweater and tuck them away. In the wardrobe, your grey jacket, which I forced you to take, embraces its hanger forlornly. I touch it with the gaze of a lover who gave you everything. It was never enough.

I emerge into the fragrant evening to touch the coarse bark and embrace our favorite tree trunk. Your ashes lay buried beneath my feet. The old oak offers us shelter.

Desperately needing solace, I stay with you in the blackness.

Nobody knows my body the way you do. I become a happy child surrendering to your warmth when you, the older more confident lover, roll over and curl up behind me. Your shape fits mine. We are joined at the hip, covered in sweat and glued together. At such moments, no gods in heaven nor powers on earth could tear us apart.

They count wet tentacles, my moving fingers. Though I stretch my open arms in the under-tow, I am not able to reach you. The river is an elegant spiral, swarming with fish and silky moss. On the banks of a pool I plant a note of hope: *I am free when I love!*

It seems we start the journey from opposite directions. *I want a cuddle,* you plead like a child, but I'm scared and want to flee. Whatever they did to you and whatever they did to me, we invariably end up in a hopeless collision. You assure me you are brave and will never give up. I mostly bleed.

You were still in bed when I recklessly pulled off the blankets. Your rising and falling hairy chest exposed a vulnerability I had not anticipated. You shivered and abruptly turned away, whispering into your hands, as if you wanted to warm them up. But I could not hear what you were saying.

At the beginning I worried about my mistakes. Complicated puzzles unwittingly crept into my speech. I was so embarrassed. The meaning, which was difficult to understand, competed with the awkwardness of our touching hands. Familiarity softened uneasiness. Now, with my feverish palaver, I conceal what should be revealed.

In the space of flashing dreams I notice a muffled hint. Sleep is not giving me any hope of rest beneath a waterfall of pulled-down blinds that soften the light. I could untie myself from the warm cover, but I toss about in bed, promising myself the gift of a peaceful day. Then I'll offer you an indulgence which you'll pounce on with impatience.

We quarreled as usual because we couldn't find a better reason for silence. Palpable threat was in the air when you pushed me away. Wrapped in a cloak of veiled rage, you walked out into the freezing cold, leaving an open book on a messy bed. A cast-off glove covered the left-hand page; the right, a line from a poem on yellowing paper: *One day, after kissing, he did not leave**.

*by Hafis

I'm embraced afresh by the kindness of silence, stunned and unprepared. Loneliness is only a mirror-image of closeness. Sometimes I feel it stronger when you sleep alone, remote and exhausted in the other room. More violently when your lips almost touch the strained membrane of my inner ear. Then you keep stubbornly quiet.

We were having a quiet cup of coffee. You seemed indifferent and cold. Suddenly we heard a tremendous thump against the windowpane and ran upstairs. A young blackbird lay upon the window sill in shock with its beak wide open taking shallow breaths in agony. I thought you'd be distressed about the broken glass. I was mistaken. To my surprise you really cared about the bird.

The next day we heard a similar thump. I jumped. There was no doubt about what had happened. We remained seated, held our breath and counted endless seconds in silence. We hoped the bird would revive and fly away. On the terrace, a sparrow lay on its back, its stiff legs protruding, head turned to one side.

Day and night I write sentences with semen on the surface of your skin. This act is as elusive as our manuscript, which is never complete. Sometimes I tire of searching for the right word. Then I come back and try to delve deeper. When I find solutions closer to the core of my obsession will I be at ease.

I will shelter your meadow with a thicket of wilderness, draw grey hair on your temples and a tuft-like tail on the butt of a pursued buck. I will pleasure my impatient stag, grazing sweet grass in the pastures of a hidden valley, where nobody can find you. I keep wondering how you are going to catch me when your lovely hoofs wear out, running up our hill.

The walls along the streets and boulevards are crumbling with astonishing ease. Without complaining, carved statues fall on their knees and sit on pavements covered in moss. The search for a roof over our heads *which I have known from the beginning* can finally end. Tranquility resides in the rooms of our house. I hear it coming from every floor. Upstairs, downstairs and within.

Hearing a Beethoven piano concerto and the shrieks of crazy birds, I dive into a raging storm. Bullets of hail riddle my skin. Thunder strikes every single bone. Fierce rain purifies my soul as all my doubts and fear go up in flames.

An eruption of anger assaults my being. I shout with a raised fist: *Fuck them, Ludwig. Fuck them!*

A Midsummer Night's Press is an independent poetry press. It's imprints include, among others:

Body Language: devoted to poetry exploring questions of gender and sexual identity: *This is What Happened in Our Other Life* by Achy Obejas, *Banalities* by Brane Mozetic (translated by Elizabeta Zargi with Timothy Liu), *Handmade Love* by Julie R. Enszer, *Mute* by Raymond Luczak, *Milk and Honey: A Celebration of Jewish Lesbian Poetry* edited by Julie R. Enszer, *Dialectic of the Flesh* by Roz Kaveney, *Fortunate Light* by David Bergman, *Deleted Names* by Lawrence Schimel, *When I Was Straight* by Julie Marie Wade, *This Life Now* by Michael Broder, *Our Lady of the Crossword* by Rigoberto González, *The Sexy Storm* by Edward van de Vendel (translated by David Colmer) and *Same-Sexy Marriage* by Julie Marie Wade.

Periscope: devoted to poetry in translation by women writers: *One is None* by Estonian poet Kätlin Kaldmaa (translated by Miriam McIlfatrick), *Anything Could Happen* by Slovenian poet Jana Putrle (translated by Barbara Jursa), *Dissection* by Spanish poet Care Santos (translated by Lawrence Schimel), *Caravan Lullabies* by Lithuanian poet Ilze Butkute (translated by Rimas Uzgiris) and *Having Never Met* by Latvian poet Inga Pizane (translated by Jayde Will).